Frog Report

Greg Pyers

Contents

**Red-eyed
tree frog**

Frogs

Have you ever touched a frog?
If you have, you would
know that frogs have cool,
moist skin. Frogs are **amphibians**.

**Strawberry
poison frog**

This means they spend part of their lives
in water and part on land. Frogs can be
found in ponds, streams, swamps, forests,
marshes, and rain forests. Frogs live on
every **continent** except Antarctica.

Marsupial frogs

Have you ever heard a frog? Some frogs croak and some chirp like birds. One kind of frog makes a sound like the engine of a motorbike. Frogs have been singing in their watery homes since the time of the dinosaurs.

This small frog croaks loudly.

Frogs in Trouble

There aren't as many frogs in the world as there used to be. Many types of frogs have become **extinct**. They no longer exist anywhere on Earth.

Scientists first became aware that frogs were in trouble about 25 years ago. Places that had many frogs one year had hardly any frogs the next year. Some places had no frogs at all. What was happening to the frogs? What was making them disappear?

Scientists study the places where frogs live to find out why some frogs are disappearing.

When scientists began studying the problem, they learned that many things were hurting the frogs. Frogs are easily hurt by changes to their **habitat**, or the place where they live. It is difficult for frogs to survive when the **wetlands** where they live are destroyed or become **polluted**.

It is difficult for frogs to live in a polluted pond.

Frogs are very sensitive to pollution and to **disease** because they have thin, moist skin. Frogs **absorb**, or take in, water through their skin. If the water where they live is polluted, the frogs absorb any poisons in the water.

A frog's thin skin doesn't protect it from poisons.

Frogs around the world are being affected by changes in their habitats. Let's look at some frogs from China, the United States, and Australia. We'll see what is happening to them, and what is being done to save them.

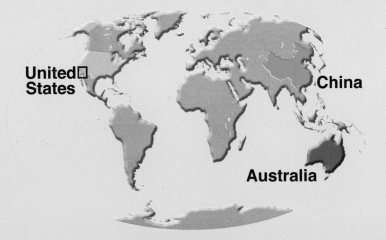

United States

China

Australia

Frog Log

Romer's Tree Frog

Romer's tree frog is a tiny frog that is less than an inch long. This frog only lives in a few forests in China. Romer's tree frogs don't live anywhere else on Earth.

In the 1980s, much of this frog's forest habitat was cut down to make way for an airport. The Romer's tree frogs were in danger. Something had to be done.

Scientists rescued 30 frogs and took them to a zoo. Soon, the zoo had **bred** hundreds of frogs. Scientists from the zoo released these frogs into special forests that had been set aside for them. By breeding more frogs and by **conserving**, or saving, their forest habitat, scientists were able to save this frog.

A scientist releases Romer's tree frogs into a special forest set aside for the frogs.

California Red-Legged Frog

The California red-legged frog was once common in the state it was named for. It is now very rare. Pollution is one of the main things harming this kind of frog.

Pesticides are chemicals used to kill insects, rats, and other pests that damage crops. These pesticides can pollute the streams where the frogs live. Frogs absorb the pesticides through their skin. The pesticides make the frogs sick. They often don't survive.

Scientists breed California red-legged frogs in zoos.

Scientists are working with farmers to reduce the amount of pesticides used where the frogs live. They are also breeding California red-legged frogs in zoos and releasing them into clean streams. By breeding more frogs and reducing the pollution in the frogs' habitat, scientists are hoping they will save this kind of frog.

Southern Corroboree Frog

Thousands of southern corroboree frogs used to live in wetland areas high in the mountains in Australia. Today, fewer than 200 of these frogs survive. This habitat is far from cities. There is no pollution. Why are the frogs disappearing?

Scientists discovered that a disease is killing these frogs. The disease spreads from frog to frog. It makes the frogs' skin dry out, causing the frogs to die.

Scientists are planning to breed southern corroboree frogs in zoos. They are also testing mountain habitats to find out which areas are free of the deadly disease. The scientists will release the frogs into safe mountain areas.

Scientists look for southern corroboree frogs to study.

Saving Frogs

Scientists are working to save frogs. By learning more about frogs and their habitats, we can protect the wetlands they need to survive. When we hear frogs singing in their homes, it's a sign that their habitat is healthy and the frogs are here to stay.

Glossary

absorb	to soak up
amphibian	an animal that spends part of its life in water and part on land
breed	to produce or raise offspring
conserve	to protect or save something
continent	one of seven largest bodies of land on Earth
disease	something that makes a living thing sick
extinct	no longer exists on Earth
habitat	the place where a plant or animal usually lives
pesticide	a chemical used to destroy harmful insects and other pests
pollute	to make land, air, or water unclean
wetland	an area of land that is covered with water

Index